# EVE RICE

# City Night

## pictures by PETER SIS

Greenwillow Books  New York

The full-color artwork, oil paintings, was
mechanically separated and reproduced in four colors.
The typeface is Avant Garde Gothic Book and Medium.

Printed in Hong Kong by South China Printing Co.
First Edition   10 9 8 7 6 5 4 3 2 1

Library of Congress Cataloging-in-Publication Data
Rice, Eve.     City night.
Summary: An illustrated poem depicting the
beauty and diversity of a city at night.
1. City and town life—Juvenile poetry.
2. Night—Juvenile poetry.
3. Children's poetry, American.
[1. City and town life—Poetry.
2. Night—Poetry.     3. American poetry]
I. Sís, Peter, ill.     II. Title.
PS3568.I276C5   1987     811'.54     86-12021
ISBN 0-688-06856-1
ISBN 0-688-06857-X (lib. bdg.)

For Tim, with love
—E. R.

To Ava
—P. S.

The city lights
up at night.
Going.
Glowing.
Yellow.
Bright!

City dresses
up so fine.
Sparkle.
Spangle.
Jangle.
Shine!

Then
bing,
bang,
bong!
City singing.
Rustling.
Rumbling.
Roaring.
Ringing!

On stage,
off stage,
city clapping.
Laughing.
Cheering.
Fingers
snapping.

Razzle, dazzle,
city dancing.
Jostling.
Jumping.
Pawing.
Prancing.

Simmer, sizzle,
city munching.
Grinding.
Grilling.
Crackling.
Crunching.

Till
tick,
tock,
tock...

Someone
somewhere
sleeping
tight.

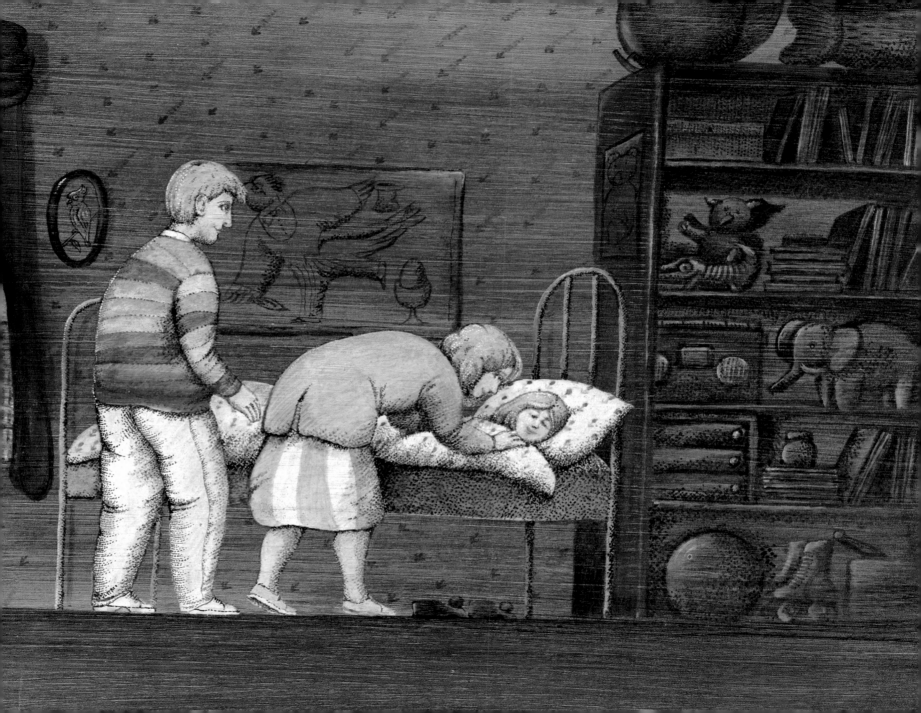

Stacking,
packing.
City yawning.
Snuggling.
Snoring...

Sun is dawning.